ROALD DAHL

ROTSOME & REPULSANT WORDS

Original text by
Roald Dahl

Illustrated by
Quentin Blake

Compiled by
Susan Rennie

WARNING:

NOT for polite
and well-mann
chiddle

INTRODUCTION

Have you noticed how some grown-ups use the same rude words and phrases *over and over again*? Most grown-ups think there are only a few rude words in the world. But in fact there are **squillions** of them — and the best ones are the ones you make up yourself, as only you know what they *really mean*.

We have gathered together the most outrageously **rotsome** and **repulsant** words from Roald Dahl's stories — and in case you run out of those, we will also show you how to create your own. (Note that you won't find the REALLY rude words here that Farmer Bunce shouts at Mr Fox. Those are SO RUDE that many grown-ups have never heard of them either.)

No one is suggesting that you run about cursing like a giant all day long. How very boring that would be!

For just like Magic Fingers, rude words have a strange power that comes from saving them up to use *at just the right time*.

Roald Dahl made up more **redunculously** rude words than any other writer. So learn from the best. The grown-ups will never know.

— Susan Rennie

CONTENTS

HOW TO curse LIKE A giant

Giant curses sound a bit like grown-up curses, but no one knows exactly what they mean, so it is perfectly fine to print them in a book, or to say them out loud.

bopmuggered *adjective*

If a giant says he is *bopmuggered*, he is in a very sticky situation and is NOT HAPPY about it. It is very rude to say you are *bopmuggered*, which is why giants like to say it.

'I is bopmuggered!' screeched the Butcher Boy.—THE BFG

Other **gigantuously** rude words which mean the same thing are:

crodsquinkled   gunzleswiped
fluckgungled   slopgroggled
flushbunkled   splitzwiggled
goosegruggled   swogswalloped

Well, I'll be fluckgungled!

Giants are also experts at HURLING INSULTS at each other.
Here are some of their best ones.

Squinky little squiddler!

Prunty little pogswizzler!

Piffling little swishfiggler!

grobsquiffler *noun*

If you call someone a *grobsquiffler*, you are saying they are silly and not important.

'Now then, you little

grobsquiffler!'

boomed the Fleshlumpeater.

—THE BFG

pogswizzler and **swishfiggler** *nouns*

Pogswizzler and *swishfiggler* are very rude names that the **horrigust** giants call the BFG.

squinky squiddler *noun*

Something *squinky* is small and unimportant.
It is very rude to call someone *squinky*, and
even more rude to call them a **squinky squiddler**.

troggy *adjective* **troggier, troggiest**

Something *troggy* is vile and horrible.
Troggy is a very strong word, so only
troggy giants use it as an insult.

*The giants picked up rocks and hurled them
after him. He managed to dodge them. 'Ruddy
little runt!' they shouted. 'Troggy little twit!'*
—THE BFG

MAKE UP YOUR OWN
gigantuous CURSE WORD

Mix the start of one giant rude word with the end of a different one to make a rude word that *no* **human bean** *has ever heard before.*

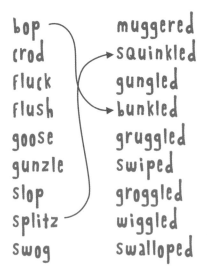

bop	muggered
crod	squinkled
fluck	gungled
flush	bunkled
goose	gruggled
gunzle	swiped
slop	groggled
splitz	wiggled
swog	swalloped

Rotsome words are very flexible (a bit like **Vermicious Knids**). You can bend them into other types of word that sound *even rotsomer.*

You can make any of these **gigantuous** curse words into INSULTS or EXPLETIVES.

I'mbopbunkled!

We're splitzsquinkled!

For example, if a beastly grown-up calls you:

You squinky little crodsquinkle!

You could reply:

You ghastly grown-up gunzleswipe!

Or a giant who is RAGING (because you have fed him a snozzcumber), might say:

Swogswallopers!

or even

Bopmuggerly swogswallopers!

!!ROTSOME TIP!!

An EXPLETIVE is what you say out loud when you are REALLY annoyed about something. It is not the same as an INSULT, as you are not saying it to anyone in particular.

See Explosive Expletives on page 56.

HOW TO INSULT LIKE A Trunchbull

'You ignorant little slug!' *the Trunchbull bellowed.*

'You witless weed! You empty-headed hamster! You stupid glob of glue!'

—MATILDA

Miss Trunchbull likes nothing better than to insult her pupils, and she uses some clever techniques to make her insults even more effective.

You ignorant little slug!

A *slug* is a small, soft animal that looks like a snail but has no shell.

You festering gumboil!

A *gumboil* is a painful swelling caused by an infected tooth. (It is important NOT to confuse it with a *gumball*, which is a hard ball of chewing gum — as only one of them is nice to chew.)

You fleabitten fungus!

A *fungus* is a plant without leaves or flowers that grows best in dark, moist places. Mushrooms and toadstools are types of fungus.

13

Here are some other things that make **slimacious** insults:

SNOZZCUMBER

SEMOLINA BLANCMANGE MUCUS FROGSPAWN

GLOOP

!!ROTSOME TIP!!
Note that *mucus* is a noun, but *mucous* is an adjective, so you would say: *You mucous mound of mucus!*

Trunchbull Technique no.2: Use alliteration

Alliteration is when you use the same **Lovely Letter Lots** of times.

You clotted carbuncle!
You witless weed!

carbuncle *noun*

A *carbuncle* is a large swollen boil on your skin, so to call someone a *carbuncle* is not nice at all, which is why Miss Trunchbull likes to say it—even though she is the most Beastly Carbuncle of them all.

Trunchbull Technique no.3: BELLOW!

There is no point in coming up with a **rotsomely** good insult if no one can hear it. Think of what you are going to say. Then take a **gigantuous** breath, and . . . **BELLOW!!**

Instant Insult-Maker

Try using this formula to make your own Trunchbull-isms. It works best if you use alliteration—and remember to BELLOW!

You ⟨ *adjective* ⟩ ⟨ *noun* ⟩ of ⟨ *noun* ⟩

Examples: You **big blob** of **blancmange**!
You **glutinous glob** of **glue**!

HOW TO BE AS Grumpy AS A Grandma

Some grandmas, like Grandma Georgina and George's grandma, get very grumpy, and it makes them feel better to curse and say rude words to show how cross they are. (In fact, cursing usually makes any grown-up feel better, which is why so many of them do it.)

Grandmothers are especially good at insults, perhaps because they have had a long time to practise. George's grandma calls him:

a disgusting little worm!

a nasty little maggot!

Charlie's Grandma Georgina doesn't trust Willy Wonka and often calls him rude names, such as **You miserable old mackerel!** It is very rude to call someone a *mackerel*, which is why she likes saying it so much.

'You miserable old mackerel!' said Grandma Georgina, sailing past him. 'Just when we start having a bit of fun, you want to stop it!'
—CHARLIE AND THE GREAT GLASS ELEVATOR

ROTSOME FACT
The word *insult* means literally to 'jump on' someone. It is related to *salmon*, which means a 'leaping fish'.

HOW TO BE rude backwards
(the ESIO TROT way)

If you've read *Esio Trot*, you'll know that **Saying Things Backwards** is essential for communicating with tortoises. For example:

Tahw a ylevol ecuttel fael!
=
What a lovely lettuce leaf!

18

But saying things backwards is also a **redunculously** good way of saying **EDUR SDROW** without grown-ups noticing (unless they can speak Tortoise of course).

This technique works best in small doses (like **Wonka-Vite**). If you use it too often, grown-ups might crack the code, and then you will be in **GIB ELBUORT**.

mub → Example: Miss Trunchbull has a **gib mub!**

ylgu → Example: Aunt Sponge is **ylurt ylgu!**

yllis → Example: The President is a **yrev yllis nam!**

19

HOW TO SPEAK MIDEOUS Martian
(THE WILLY WONKA WAY)

When Willy Wonka pretends to be a Martian, he makes up a string of **redunculous** words to shout at the President of the United States (who is being very silly and thoroughly deserves it). He is therefore able to be very rude without the President (or his Chief Interpreter) having a clue what he is saying.

You can try this, too, either to the President or to another grown-up who is being equally silly. When they don't understand you, just tell them you are speaking Martian.

Mideous Martian technique no. 1: YUBEE LUNI!

This a very useful Martian phrase for telling a President or other grown-up that they are being silly.

Charlie's eyes were riveted on Mr Wonka.
. . . He put so much force into his voice
that the effort lifted him right up on to the
tips of his toes.

'BUNGO BUNI DAFU DUNI YUBEE LUNI!'

—CHARLIE AND THE
GREAT GLASS ELEVATOR

You can make your own variations on this, by using a different Martian word after **YUBEE**. For example:

YUBEE SILI BILEE
YUBEE KRAZI PREZI DENTEE

Mideous Martian technique no. 2: ZOONK!

ZOONK is probably a very rude word in Martian, although no one knows exactly what it means. It is best to say it many times over, as fast and as loud as possible.

The next time Mr Wonka spoke, the words came out so fast and sharp and loud they were like bullets from a machine-gun.
'ZOONK-ZOONK-ZOONK-ZOONK-ZOONK!'
he barked.
—CHARLIE AND THE GREAT
GLASS ELEVATOR

An interesting variation is to say **ZOONK** at the
end of every phrase, in a threatening manner.

*Mr Wonka paused dramatically for a few seconds.
Then he took an enormous deep breath and in
a wild and fearsome voice, he yelled out:*

'KITIMBIBI ZOONK!

FUMBOLEEZI ZOONK!

GUGUMIZA ZOONK!

FUMIKAKA ZOONK!

ANAPOLALA ZOONK!

ZOONK ZOONK!'

—CHARLIE AND THE GREAT
GLASS ELEVATOR

HOW TO BE rude IN OTHER LANGUAGES

(SO GROWN-UPS WON'T NOTICE)

For centuries, grown-ups have used **rude** and **rotsome** words from other languages to curse and insult each other, so that people wouldn't know what they *really* meant. You can do this too.

Learning **rotsome** words in other languages is ESPECIALLY useful if your grown-ups have already looked up all the rude words in the *Oxford Roald Dahl Dictionary*. But they won't find these words there, so they will be thoroughly **biffsquiggled** when you use them.

beschwipsduselt *adjective*
(say bee-**shwips**-dooz-elt)
a word said by German
giants when they've had
too much to drink

furripanchoso *adjective*
(say furry-pan-**choh**-zoh)
a word said by Spanish giants
which has nothing to do with
furry sizzlepans

gulliewullied *adjective*
a word said by Scottish giants
which has something to do
with being stuck in a bog

gurke

which means **sickable cucumber.**

In Italian it is a **cetrionzolo** (say chet-ree-on-**zoh**-loh), which means **very odd cucumber.**

In Spanish it is a **pepináspero** (say pep-ee-**na**-spe-roh), which means **sour cucumber.**

In Scots it is a **feechcumber**, which translates as **yuck-cumber.**

Troggy TERMS FOR Twits
(AND OTHER BEASTLY BEINGS)

Mr and Mrs Twit are **mideously** mean to each other (and even worse to children and animals). They love to call each other NASTY NAMES, such as

grizzly old grunion!
rotten old turnip!
Filthy old frumpet!

Mrs Twit . . . suddenly called out at the top of her voice,
'Here I come, you grizzly old **grunion**! *You rotten old* **turnip**!
You filthy old **frumpet**!'
—THE TWITS

frumpet *noun*

If you call someone a *frumpet*, you mean that they are old
and unattractive. It is very mean to call someone a **frumpet**,
which is why Mrs Twit enjoys saying it.

* * ROTSOME FACT * *

The word *frumpet* may be based on *frump*, which has a
similar meaning and comes from an older word *frumple*
meaning 'wrinkle'.

grunion *noun*

A *grunion* is a very mean or grumpy
person. George also calls his
grandmother a **grizzly old grunion**.

Mrs Twit could have used these other **vegetibbles** to describe her husband, too:

frumpkin *noun*

A *frumpkin* is a vegetable used to make *frumpkin pie*. Unlike the **snozzcumber**, it is good to eat and its name suggests it looks or tastes a bit like a pumpkin.

wurzel *noun*

A *wurzel* is a yellow root vegetable that is fed to farm animals. It is very rude to call someone a **wurzel** (or worse, a **snozzcumber**).

You frumptious old frumpkin!

You silly snozzcumber!

You wizened old wurzel!

Warning! It is never a good idea to call a

GIANT

a silly Snozz(umber

unless you have
a very good escape plan
(such as hiding inside a
Snozz(umber).

grinksludger *noun*
A *grinksludger* is a mean and nasty person, like the *grinksludging* Farmers Boggis, Bunce and Bean.

nincompoop *noun*
A *nincompoop* is a very silly person, such as Augustus Gloop, the *great big greedy nincompoop.*

the great big greedy

rotrasper *noun*

A *rotrasper* is a thoroughly beastly grown-up, like Mrs Clonkers or Miss Trunchbull.

'She locked us in the dark cellar for a day and a night without anything to eat or drink.' 'The rotten old rotrasper!' cried the BFG.

— THE BFG

!!ROTSOME TIP!!
Try rolling the R sound at the start of a word like RRRRROTRASPER until you sound like the Grrrrrand High Witch. This will make your curses and insults sound more menacing.

incompoop

squeakpip *noun*

A *squeakpip* is a very unimportant and silly grown-up.

'Human beans is thinking they is very clever, but they is not.
They is nearly all of them notmuchers and squeakpips.'
—THE BFG

squifflerotter *noun*

A *squifflerotter* is a mean and nasty grown-up.

'Grown-up human beans is not famous for their kindnesses.
They is all squifflerotters and grinksludgers.'
—THE BFG

vermicious *adjective*

Something *vermicious* is vicious and nasty, just like a Knid.

'It's worse than that!' cried the Chief of Police. 'It's a vermicious
Knid! Oh, just look at its vermicious gruesome face!'
—JAMES AND THE GIANT PEACH

The VERY BAD dreams
that the BFG catches are called bogthumpers, grobswitchers and trogglehumpers.

These also make good names
for mean human beans.

Examples: Aunt Spiker is a rotten
old **grobswitcher!**

Miss Trunchbull is a mean
and nasty **bogthumper!**

ROTSOME FACT
It's not just Knids that are vermicious!
The word *vermicious* means 'worm-like',
which is exactly how George's
grandma describes him.

Repulsant WORDS FOR ROTSOME THINGS

Have you ever come across something as *filthsomely foul* as Mr Twit's beard? Or as *oozingly icky* as Farmer Bunce's doughnuts? There are lots of truly revolting things in Roald Dahl's stories, but he never runs out of words to describe them. Take **snozzcumbers**, for example:

'It's disgusterous!' the BFG gurgled. 'It's sickable!
It's rotsome! It's maggotwise! Try it yourself,
this foulsome snozzcumber!'
—THE BFG

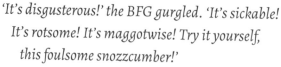

!!ROTSOME TIP!!
The word *disgusterous* starts with *disgusting* but has a different ending which makes you think of *dangerous* or *murderous*, as if snozzcumbers taste like deadly poison.

All these words mean 'digusting' or 'repulsive' and perfectly describe a **snozzcumber** or other **rotsome** things.

bogrotting
disgusterous
filthsome
foulsome

grizzling
grobswitchy
icky-poo
maggotwise
muckfrumping

repulsant
rotsome
sickable
ucky-mucky
uckyslush

Be snozzcumbersome!

You can also make your own words based on **snozzcumber** to describe something **disgusterous**. For example:

That's the most

snozzcumberish, snozzcumberous, snozzcumbersome, snozzcumberumptious

thing I've ever tasted!

Rotsome THINGS

grimesludge *noun*
Grimesludge is thick and
dirty mud.

*'By goggles,' he said, taking
the jar out of the suitcase,
'your head is not quite so full of
grimesludge after all!'*
—THE BFG

slubber *noun*
Slubber is a kind of
muddy sludge found
in boggy places.

slutch *noun*
Slutch is anything that looks or tastes
revolting, like a bite of **snozzcumber**.

*'That is the most disgusterous taste that
is ever clutching my teeth! You must be
buggles to be swalloping slutch like that!'*
—THE BFG

swatchwallop *noun*
Swatchwallop is the most disgusting
thing you can imagine eating.

*'By goggles!' he cried. 'This stuff is making
snozzcumbers taste like swatchwallop!'*
—THE BFG

38

Roald Dahl once said:

If you have good thoughts they will shine out of your face like sunbeams and you will always look lovely. —THE TWITS

To make this apply to **TWITS**, **WITCHES** or other beastly beings, just use the opposite words:

If you have ~~good~~ **BAD** thoughts they will ~~shine out of~~ **OOZE FROM** your face like ~~sunbeams~~ **SLIME** and you will always look ~~lovely~~ **REPULSANT**.

Even rotsomer!

You can add the endings **–er** and **–est** to a **rotsome** word to make your own COMPARATIVE or SUPERLATIVE. For example:

That cheese is **rotsomer** *than a snozzcumber.*

Farmer Bean is the **squifflerottenest** *human bean ever!*

REDUNCULOUS
WORDS FOR RATHER
RUDE
THINGS

'If everyone is making whizzpoppers, then why not talk about it?'—THE BFG

bottom noun

Your bottom is the part of your body that you sit on. **Vermicious Knids** have pointy bottoms which are not very good for sitting but make good weapons.

'Hello, you great Knid! Tell us, how do you do?
You're a rather strange colour today.
Your bottom is purple and lavender blue.
Should it really be looking that way?
—CHARLIE AND THE GREAT GLASS ELEVATOR

Some grown-ups try to avoid saying the word **bottom**, even though it is a perfectly sensible word. They use all sorts of **redunculous** words instead, which mean the same thing, like *posterior*. They will even say it in French, calling it a *derrière* (which rhymes with *were*).

41

Some other words for 'bottom' you will find in Roald Dahl's stories are:

BEHIND   REAR   RUMP

Mrs Salt . . . was now kneeling right on the edge of the hole with her head down and her enormous behind sticking up in the air like a giant mushroom.

—CHARLIE AND THE CHOCOLATE FACTORY

I sat. I screamed. I jumped a foot!
Would you believe that I had put
That tender little rump of mine
Upon a giant porcupine!

—DIRTY BEASTS

Oh, K-nids' K-nickers!

42

knickers *plural noun*

Knickers are underpants for girls or women.
The word is a short form of *knickerbockers*,
a type of knee-length trousers named after
Diedrich *Knickerbocker*, a character in an
American story.

* * ROTSOME FACT * *

In the 1940s, underpants were sometimes
made from recycled parachute silk. They
were called *parapants*.

*As she floated gently down, Mrs Twit's petticoat billowed out
like a parachute, showing her long knickers.*

—THE TWITS

Note that the phrase **Knids' Knickers** is NOT
alliterative, as *Knid* is pronounced with a K at the
start (just like the words *knight* and *knock* used
to be). To make it more fun AND alliterative,
why not pronounce both words with a K?

43

whizzpopper *noun*

A *whizzpopper* is the noise that comes out of your bottom when you drink too much fizzy **frobscottle**. (It even happens to the Queen.) It is not a rude word (or sound) to giants—just to **human beans**.

'I has Her Majester's permission!' cried the BFG, and all at once he let fly with a whizzpopper that sounded as though a bomb had exploded in the room.

— THE BFG

In giant languages around the world,
whizzpoppers are called:

flitspoppers (Dutch)

furzelbäume (German)

popotraques (Spanish)

rummlypumps (Scots)

* * ROTSOME FACT * *

The word *whizzpopper* is ONOMATOPOEIC,
which means that it sounds like the thing it
describes. Some old words for *whizzpoppers* are
squib, *poot* and *crackeret*.

Time-twiddling Curses

In Giant Country, a *time-twiddler* is someone who lives for a **gigantuously** long time (as all giants do). A time-twiddling word is one that is very old, too, or that was used long ago.

Here are some time-twiddling curses and insults that were said by cross human beans long long ago. Some of them sound just like words you might hear in Giant Country!

bescumber *verb*

To *bescumber* is an old word which means 'to poo upon' someone. If you are VERY BRAVE, you could say to the Grand High Witch:

May bats bescumber you!

But be warned: although it will be great fun, it may well be the last thing you will ever say.

46

dunderhead *noun*

A *dunderhead* is a very stupid person. Charles Dickens once described a characer as the *dunderheaded king of the noodles* — so you could say that Mr Twit is the **dunderheaded king of Squiggly Spaghetti!** And talking of pasta . . . the word *macaroni* also used to mean a *dunderhead* or very silly grown-up.

* * ROTSOME FACT * *
Charles Dickens was a favourite author of both Roald Dahl and the BFG. The BFG's name for him is *Dahl's Chickens.*

flibbertigibbet *noun*

A *flibbertigibbet* is someone who won't stop chattering. It is an *onomatopoeic* word, which sounds like what it means.

If you say *flibbertigibbet* over and over again, you will start to sound like one!

fopdoodle _noun_

A _fopdoodle_ is an old word for a very silly person. If Mr and Mrs Twit had lived hundreds of years ago, they would have been called Mr and Mrs _Fopdoodle_. Note that this word is not related to **whangdoodle** (a terrifying creature from Loompaland) or to **bunkdoodle** (which means to give you nightmares), although it is possible to say:

That fopdoodle has been

ninnyhammer _noun_

Hundreds of years ago, silly people were called _ninnyhammers_. This would be a splendid insult for Miss Trunchbull to use, because her favourite sport is throwing the hammer (as well as throwing children with pigtails).

numbskull *noun*

A *numbskull* is someone whose head is emptier than a **bundongle**. You could also call them a **cloudbrain** — but be careful not to say this to Cloud-men, or they will get very angry and hurl hailstones down at you.

bunkdoodled by a whangdoodle!

slubberdegullion *noun*

A *slubberdegullion* is someone who is very sloppy and messy, so it is a perfect word for Mr Twit. It comes from an even older word, to *slubber*, meaning 'to smear'.

zoodikers!

This ancient curse word sounds like something Willy Wonka would say to the President.
You could also say **zookers**, **zoonters** or just **zooks!**

49

Zooks! What a slubberdegullion!

Words that turn UPSIDE DOWN (slowly)

Twits are not the only things that turn upside down! Did you know that a word can start off as a perfectly nice and polite word, but then change over time to become something **not-so-nice?**

For example . . .

naughty *adjective*

The word *naughty* is related to *nought* and originally meant 'very poor'. It later came to mean 'wicked' and then just 'badly behaved'. So originally, it was poor Charlie Bucket who was *naughty*, not the greedy Augustus Gloop!

silly *adjective*

The word *silly* originally meant 'very good or worthy' and was also used as a surname. In the Middle Ages, being called Mr or Mrs *Silly* was like being called Mr or Mrs *Good* (not Mr or Mrs Twit).

BUT ON THE OTHER HAND...

nice *adjective*

The word *nice* originally meant 'silly or foolish' — not pleasant at all! In other words, long long ago, Mrs Twit would have been a very *nice* person.

Extra-usually Silly Similes

When you describe something by comparing it to something else, you are using a SIMILE.

'You is only interested in guzzling human beans.' 'And you is dotty as a dogswoggler!' cried the Bloodbottler.
—THE BFG

Similes make splendiferous insults, especially ones that use alliteration. Here are some similes that Roald Dahl uses to describe someone as slightly dotty:

as **batty** as a **bullfrog**

as **crazy** as a **crumpet**

as **dotty** as a **doughnut**

as **potty** as a **pilchard**

as **quacky** as a **duckhound**

as **dotty** as a **dogswoggler**

You can use the same techniques to make up your own dotty, silly similes. For an **extra-redunculous** simile, choose something that is spotted or dotty already for your comparison:

> as **dotty** as a **currant bun**
> as **dotty** as a **Dalmatian**
> as **dotty** as a **Pink-Spotted Scrunch**
> as **dotty** as a **Spotted Whangdoodle**

Not all similes have to be dotty however! You can turn any **extra-usual** creature or **redunculous** object into a silly simile.

> as **crazy** as a **cockatootloo**
> as **fussy** as a **fogglefrump**
> as **grubby** as a **grobblesquirt**
> as **quacky** as a **quogwinkle**
> as **silly** as a **sizzlepan**

Explosive expletives

An *expletive* (say eks-**plee**-tiv) is a word you say when you are
Very Cross Indeed about something. You may have heard
grown-ups using expletives when they stub their toe or spill
frobscottle on the carpet.

Here are some expletives that Roald Dahl invented, which will
NOT get you into trouble with grown-ups, because they won't
have heard of them before. (In fact, they might start using
them, too.)

Gunghummers and bogswinkles!

*A shower of glass fell upon the poor BFG. 'Gunghummers and
bogswinkles!' he cried. 'What was that?'*

—THE BFG

The BFG also says:

Oh mince my maggots!
and
Oh swipe my swoggles!

But no one knows exactly
what his *swoggles* are, or
how to swipe them—which
is probably just as well.

Great whistling whangdoodles!

This is one of Willy Wonka's favourite expletives. As **redunculous** things are always happening to Mr Wonka, he invents explosive expletives (as well as exploding sweets), so that he always has something to shout.

A *whangdoodle* is a terrifying creature that eats Oompa-Loompas. It is NOT the same as a *wangdoodle*, which is a *delumptious* sweet. (But if you give a *whangdoodle* a *wangdoodle*, it might stop eating Oompa-Loompas for a while.)

Great Whistling

Snorting snozzwangers!

This is another favourite expression of Willy Wonka. A *snozzwanger* is a deadly three-footed creature that lives in Loompaland and preys on Oompa-Loompas

'Snorting snozzwangers!'
he yelled, picking himself up
and waving the letter about
as though he were swatting
mosquitoes.

—CHARLIE AND THE
GREAT GLASS ELEVATOR

Vhangdoodles!

!!ROTSOME TIP!!
You can use any word that grown-ups do not understand as an expletive or other rude word.
For example, try saying:
Oh, FOGGLEFRUMPS!
or
What a load of BUNGSWOGGLE!

A LOAD of ... Poppyrot

All these words mean 'silly nonsense or rubbish'. They are very useful if someone (usually a grown-up) has said something that does not make sense — such as absolutely everything that Matilda's parents say.

balderdash *noun* (say **bol**-der-dash)
'Ridiculous!' they shouted. 'Absurd!'
'Poppycock!' 'Balderdash!' 'Madness!'
—JAMES AND THE GIANT PEACH

bunkum *noun*

'It's tying us up like a parcel!' yelled Grandma Josephine. 'Bunkum!' said Mr Wonka.

—CHARLIE AND THE GREAT
GLASS ELEVATOR

piffle *noun*

'Cut the piffle, Shanks,' snapped the President. 'This is a national emergency!'

—CHARLIE AND THE GREAT GLASS ELEVATOR

ROTSOME FACT
The word *bunkum* is based on a place called *Buncombe* in North America, which once had a politician who wouldn't stop talking.

poppycock *noun*

'You', said Mr Fox, 'are going to be poisoned.' 'Poppycock!' said Rat.

—FANTASTIC MR FOX

ROTSOME FACT
The word *poppycock* comes from Dutch *pappekak*, which means literally 'soft poo'.

twaddle *noun* (rhymes with *waddle*)

School teachers suffer a good deal from having to listen to this sort of twaddle from proud parents.

—MATILDA

KEEP TALKING twaddle

Human beans say and think SO MANY silly things that there are never enough words to describe them all. In fact, there are as many words for 'nonsense' as there are *phizz-whizzing* sweets in Willy Wonka's factory!

Here are some more rude words that human beans and giants use to tell each other they are talking twaddle.

PIGSPIFFLE   BUGSWALLOP   POPPYROT

PIGWASH   TUMMYROT

RUBBSQUASH   SLUSHBUNGLE

ROMMYTOT   CRODSWOGGLE

The Air Marshal's face turned the colour of a ripe plum. He was not used to being told he was talking slushbungle.

—THE BFG

You can also say:

Your brain is full of bugwhiffles!

'If you will listen carefully I will try to explain,' said the BFG. 'But your brain is so full of bugwhiffles, I doubt you will ever understand.

—THE BFG

Roald Dahl made up lots of funny spoonerisms and malapropisms, like **catasterous disastrophe** and **skin and groans**. It is easy to make up your own, too, for example *belly jeans* from *jelly beans*.

!!ROTSOME TIP!!
The words *rommytot* and *tummyrot* are based on *tommyrot* (which also means 'nonsense'). *Rommytot* is a SPOONERISM (where parts of the word are swapped round), and *tummyrot* is a MALAPROPISM (a funny mistake with words).

What a load of bugswallop!

That's utter rubbsquash!

61

AND FINALLY...

Not ALL grown-ups are beastly, and not ALL human beans and creatures are *horrigust*. In fact, some are positively **buckswashling**. For every ghastly Miss Trunchbull there is a *gloriumptious* Miss Honey and for every **foulsome** Farmer Bean there is a Fantastic Mr Fox.

Roald Dahl invented lots of **not-so-rotsome** words, too, to describe *jumbly* giants, *delumptious* sweets, and other *phizz-whizzing* things.

You can find them ALL in the **fantabulous** *Oxford Roald Dahl Dictionary* . . . and of course in the splendiferous stories and poems of ROALD DAHL.